Frances Gregory Pasch

Double Vision:

Seeing God in Everyday Life Through Devotions and Poetry

Frances Gregory Pasch

Lighthouse Publishing of the Carolinas

www.lighthousepublishingofthecarolinas.com

Praise for
Double Vision: Seeing God in Everyday Life
Through Devotions and Poetry

Poignant, powerful, practical. Frances Pasch's *Double Vision* will give you a new perspective and appreciation for how God speaks to us through everyday experiences.

Marlene Bagnull
Author, Director of the Colorado and
Greater Philadelphia Christian Writers Conferences

Fran Pasch's devotions and poetry have been a blessing to me and the many readers of *The Secret Place* over the past two decades. Now they are combined for powerful daily devotional reading and reflection. Don't miss the opportunity to allow God to touch your heart through the contents of this special book.

Kathleen Hayes
Former Editor of *The Secret Place*

In *Double Vision*, Fran has written a work that will inspire you, encourage you, and stimulate you to become more like Jesus. I was so blessed reading her book, and I finished it with a sense that I had touched the heart of God. Fran's deep desire to point readers to Jesus Christ is evident throughout the work. Her transparency and vulnerability create a connection with her reader that is both powerful and compassionate. This book will make a great, life-changing gift for any occasion.

Dr. MaryAnn Diorio
Novelist, Poet, Artist and Life Coach

In *Double Vision*, Fran opens our eyes to the gifts of grace that God has left lying around in the everyday world. Her poetry will settle in your heart; her prose will awaken your mind. Read it and start to see . . . more clearly!

Rev. Jerry Scott
Senior Pastor, Faith Discovery Church

In most cases, we don't want double vision because it confuses and blurs what we want to see. Not so with Fran's volume of poems and devotions. Instead she offers clarity and beauty as we look at everyday experiences through what she calls "a double eye-opener—two ways of looking at the same spiritual truth." It's a treasure!

Patti Souder
Freelance Writer, Speaker, and Musician
Director of the Montrose Christian Writers Conference

Poetry and devotion lovers will find Fran's book inspiring and insightful.

James Watkins
Author and Speaker
www.jameswatkins.com

In a world where perspective is often distorted by the mundane, *Double Vision* lifts our eyes and gives us a glimpse of the divine.

Connie Cartisano
Author, *The Image of the Invisible*

DOUBLE VISION: SEEING GOD IN EVERYDAY LIFE THROUGH
DEVOTIONS AND POETRY BY FRANCES GREGORY PASCH
Published by Lighthouse Publishing of the Carolinas
2333 Barton Oaks Dr., Raleigh, NC, 27614

ISBN 978-1-938499-93-7
Copyright © 2013 by Frances Gregory Pasch
Cover design by Urosh Bizjak, uroshb.prosite.com and Ted Ruybal,
www.wisdomhousebooks.com
Interior design by THE FAST FINGERS, www.thefastfingers.com

Available in print from your local bookstore, online, or from the
publisher at: www.lighthousepublishingofthecarolinas.com

For more information on this book and the author visit:
www.francesgregorypasch.com

Brought to you by the creative team at
LighthousePublishingoftheCarolinas.com: Denise Loock, Eddie Jones,
Rowena Kuo, Brian Cross, and Meaghan Burnett

Library of Congress Cataloging-in-Publication Data
Pasch, Frances Gregory.
Double Vision: Seeing God in Everyday Life Through Devotions and
Poetry / Frances Gregory Pasch
1st Ed.

Printed in the United States of America

TABLE OF CONTENTS

ACKNOWLEDGMENTS

A special thank you to my husband, Jim, for his continual encouragement and unconditional love. We have been married since 1958.

Thanks to our sons—Jimmy, Glenn, Brian, Scott, and Stephen—for brightening our lives. Thanks also to our grandchildren—April, Alexandra, Rebecca, Connor, Faith, Stephen, William, Alexander, and Dillon—who bless us in so many ways.

I am especially grateful to all of the women who have attended my writers' group the past twenty-two years. Thank you for faithfully encouraging me and honestly critiquing my writing. I have learned so much from all of you and value your friendships. An extra special thanks to my writer friend, Denise Loock, for her expertise in editing this manuscript.

A thank you to my friend, Mary Hubinsky, who taught our Bible study for so many years. I treasure her dedication and encouragement.

Thank you to Marlene Bagnull, Director of the Greater Philadelphia Christian Writers Conference, and Patti Souder, Director of the Montrose Christian Writers Conference, for giving me the opportunity to meet experts in the writing field and to learn from them. I am also grateful for the friendships I have made at these conferences the past twenty-two years.

DEDICATION

I dedicate this book to my Lord and Savior,
Jesus Christ.

It is He who has gifted me with the
ability to write poems and devotions.

Abundant Life

Jesus, You have made my life
More exciting than a best seller.
The pages run the full gamut of emotion...
From joy to sorrow.
Yet in spite of circumstances,
I have been at peace with You
In every chapter of my life
For You are always there...
To enjoy the good ones with me,
To tape the torn ones together with hope,
To dry the tear-stained ones with encouragement,
To bind together with Your love
Those that come unraveled,
And to fill the empty ones
With promises of Your never ending faithfulness.
But the most exciting page of my life
Will be the last one,
When we meet face to face.

INTRODUCTION

A Double Eye-Opener

Thirty years ago, at age fifty, I began a new adventure—a personal relationship with Jesus. I had never read the Bible, so I had not made any spiritual connections with things that I had seen and heard. But once I started reading the Bible and learned more about God, I began looking at everyday happenings from a spiritual perspective too. Now, it's natural for me to look for a spiritual element in everything that takes place in my life.

In this collection of devotions, each everyday experience is coupled with a poem related to the same topic. This format becomes a double eye-opener—two ways of looking at the same spiritual truth.

I pray that once you read the analogies in this book, you too will see how enlightening your everyday activities can become. I suggest that you jot down any spiritual applications you observe in the space provided at the end of each chapter, so you don't forget what God has shown you. Who knows, you might discover that you can write devotions and poems too. At least you'll have a personal record of the many ways God reveals Himself in your daily life.

Open my eyes that I may see wonderful things in your law.
Psalm 119:18

CHAPTER 1
Beyond Our Imagination

Imagine

If when the sun shines brightly
We have to squint our eyes,
Imagine what it will be like
The day that we arise...
When God displays His Glory
For each of us to see...
His unsurpassed magnificence
For all eternity.

Face to Face

Read Revelation 19:11-16

No eye has seen, no ear has heard, no mind has conceived what God has prepared for those who love him.
1 Corinthians: 2:9

When we moved into our new home in the mountains, we discovered that water was trapped inside the thermal pane on the left side of our double back door. The water formed condensation that prevented us from seeing through the glass. The pane on the right side of the door was crystal clear and allowed us to enjoy the beautiful scenery without obstruction.

After the repairman rectified the problem by installing a new pane, we were blessed with double visibility. We were amazed at how much beauty the damaged door had obscured.

While reading my Bible one morning, I came across 1 Corinthians 13:12—"Now we see but a poor reflection as in a mirror; then we shall see face to face." Just as our problem window restricted our vision, human nature prevents us from having a clear picture of God. Our minds cannot fathom what heaven will be like, but if a clear pane of glass can make such a difference in seeing this world, imagine the splendor that will dazzle us when we meet Jesus face to face!

Prayer: Lord, we anxiously await seeing You in heaven. Amen.

Your View: Is something obscuring your picture of God today? Ask God to repair your vision.

_____
_____
_____
_____
_____

CHAPTER 2
New Creations in Christ

Full of Grace

There's a special kind of brightness
You can see upon the face
Of one who's found the Savior
And whose heart is full of grace.

There's a love that's overflowing
Coming forth from deep inside...
An outpouring of God's Spirit
Too beautiful to hide.

Transformed

Read Matthew 5:14-16

Let your light shine before men, that they may see your good deeds and praise your Father in heaven.
Matthew 5:16

One morning as I looked out my kitchen window, the white wire frames of three reindeer and a sled on my neighbor's lawn caught my eye. Her evergreens were also draped with white wire as part of her Christmas display.

In daylight, her yard wasn't that impressive, but at night her lawn was transformed into a magical fairyland. Hundreds of clear lights, not visible in sunlight, beamed in the darkness, drawing the attention of all who drove by.

Like the frame of my neighbor's lawn ornaments, we too are but a human shell, not that impressive at times. But when we ask Jesus into our lives, He plugs His life into ours. Then we shine even brighter than Christmas lights. Like my neighbor's magical fairyland, we're transformed into new creations. God's presence within us draws the attention of those who come into contact with us. Hopefully, they'll be attracted to Him by what they see in us.

Prayer: Lord, may my actions light the way so that others may be drawn to You. Amen.

Your View: What do others see when they look at you? How can you display God's brightness today?

_____
_____
_____
_____
_____

CHAPTER 3

Strength to Endure Storms

Determined

Sixty feet high atop my tree
Clings one lone leaf tenaciously.
Through raging rain and heavy snow
That tiny leaf will not let go.
I watch it and I wonder why
That it alone remains on high.
I then compare the leaf to me
And Jesus to the towering tree.
I pray that when harsh trials blow
Like the leaf I won't let go.

Hanging On

Read John 15:1-11

God is our refuge and strength, an ever-present help in trouble. Psalm 46:1

It was an exceptionally warm day for February in the Pocono Mountains in Pennsylvania. As I sat on my deck reading, I noticed that most of the trees surrounding my property were bare. Yet despite the recent heavy winds and rain, a few leaves refused to let go. They stubbornly clung to some of the spindly branches.

As Christians, we too are often faced with stormy situations. Events in our everyday lives tend to blow us in many directions. How do we react? Do we focus on the storms and let worry and fear take hold of us, or do we keep our eyes on God and cling to Him like stubborn leaves in spite of circumstances?

Just as the leaves draw strength from the tree, we gain strength from abiding in Christ. Through daily Bible study and fellowship with the Lord, we learn scriptures that we can hold on to when crises come. Instead of losing faith during trying times, like the leaves, we can cling to Christ and refuse to let go.

Prayer: Thank You, Lord, for Your promises. When I cling to them, they give me strength to face each new day. Amen.

Your View: What do you see today? The storms around you or the Savior who controls them?

_____
_____
_____
_____
_____

CHAPTER 4

Leaving Things in God's Hands

Letting Go

Why is it that I always think
That my way is the best?
Why can't I look beyond myself
And on God's shoulder rest?
Why does my stubborn nature
Want to do things its own way?
God tries so hard to teach me,
But I often go astray.
I really want to listen,
But the world's call is so strong...
It often overshadows Him,
It tempts me to belong.
But if I want His perfect peace
I must let go of "me"
And trust in Him for guidance...
Then I'll find victory.

Learning to Trust

Read Philippians 4:4-8

Trust in the Lord with all your heart and lean not on your own understanding; in all your ways acknowledge him, and he will make your paths straight. Proverbs 3:5-6

I hired a caterer for my husband's sixtieth birthday party. I picked out the menu, set the time and place, and made all the necessary arrangements. I envisioned the happy look on my husband's face on his special day.

But instead of relaxing and leaving everything in the caterer's hands, I worried. Would he come on time? Would the food be warm? Would there be enough for everyone?

Though I realize that I can't do everything myself, I find it hard to trust someone else. At times, I even have trouble leaving things in God's hands. I have surrendered my life to Him, yet many times I still want to manage everything myself.

A caterer is human and can slip up, but if I truly believe that God is who He says He is, then I shouldn't be fearful. He tells me to cast my cares on Him and to be anxious for nothing. Why should I doubt Him, when He continues to prove His faithfulness to me?

My party was successful. Everything was picture perfect: the food was delicious and beautifully displayed. The balloons and flowers added a festive touch to the room. The caterer didn't let me down. God doesn't disappoint me either. It is I who am skeptical.

Prayer: Lord, when I start to worry, remind me to look at things through Your eyes. Amen.

Your View: Are you anxious about something? How can you look beyond yourself and rest in God today?

_____
_____
_____
_____
_____

CHAPTER 5

Start Anew with God

A New Beginning

It's never too late to change your ways;
You can always start anew.
Discard those habits you're tired of
And fashion a whole new "you."

Don't consider the past a waste of time,
Just learn from your mistakes.
But if you want to forge ahead,
A change is what it takes.

So start right now and set new goals;
Decide what you want to do.
Be patient and take one step at a time,
But be sure to see each one through.

For as each step is finished
And you add it to the next,
You soon will see that you have built
A stairway to success.

Away with the Old

Read 2 Corinthians 5:17-21

Forgetting what is behind and straining toward what is ahead. Philippians 3:13

Recently, a series of messages opened my eyes to the fact that by clinging to bad habits and mindsets I wasn't experiencing God's true joy. The speaker reminded me that as a believer I have the mind of Christ. She emphasized that when I dwell on the negative rather than the positive, I block the flow of the Holy Spirit and miss out on the good things God has planned for me.

Yesterday, as I listened to one of these tapes in my car, God caught my attention in the most unexpected way. On the truck in front of me was boldly displayed the most appropriate message—"Away with the Old." Though the words actually applied to the company's refinishing process, I knew in my heart that God was saying, "Put the past behind. Start anew!"

God can use anything, even an advertisement, to communicate with us. Are we paying attention?

Prayer: Thank You, Lord, for caring enough to visually communicate with me in meaningful ways. Help me to apply, on a daily basis, what You are teaching me. Amen.

Your View: What object lesson has God used in your life recently? Look for an unexpected message today.

_____
_____
_____
_____
_____

CHAPTER 6
God Waits Expectantly

Buried Treasure

As a gardener digs deeply
Into the soil,
Help me, Lord, to dig deeply
Into Your Word.
Plant Your truths and promises
Into my heart.
Pour Your living water
Into the roots of my soul,
That I may bloom
Into a fruitful witness
To the people You bring
Into my life.

Dig In

Read Psalm 34

Taste and see that the Lord is good; blessed is the man who takes refuge in him. Psalm 34:8

"This is for you," my seven-year-old granddaughter April said as she handed me a small green dish covered with plastic wrap. "I made it myself with a recipe from my own cookbook." She beamed as she showed me the book.

As I pulled off the plastic, she said, "It's strawberry butter."

"Can I put it on toast?" I questioned.

"Yes, but you can also put it on French toast or waffles."

I thanked her, put her gift in the refrigerator, and promised to eat it with breakfast the next day. Later that night, I realized April would have been even happier if she had seen me enjoy her creation while she was still with me.

God reaches out to us in His Word and says, "Taste and see." His invitation also looks inviting, but when we put the Bible back on the shelf for a more "convenient" time, we disappoint God just as I disappointed my granddaughter.

April was excited about giving me the butter. God also waits expectantly, hoping to see us dig into His Word and take a heaping helping of His spiritual nourishment.

What better time than now!

Prayer: Lord, help me to recognize Your gentle nudges and follow through while I still have time. Amen.

Your View: Has God been nudging you to dig into His Word? Do you regularly spend time with Him?

_____
_____
_____
_____
_____

CHAPTER 7

A Clear View of God's Will

Focusing on Jesus

Today my mind is cluttered
With unimportant things...
Forgetting all the blessings
That loving Jesus brings.

Letting things take up my time
That really aren't worthwhile
Tends to make me negative
And robs me of my smile.

So if I want His perfect peace
I'll take my eyes off me,
And keep in mind His promise,
"My grace is sufficient for thee."

Clearing a Path

Read Psalm 32:8-11

I will instruct you and teach you in the way you should go; I will counsel you and watch over you. Psalm 32:8

Last winter I cleaned my messy attic. I labeled and organized the plastic boxes so it was easy to view what was inside. Seeing everything in order excited me. But during the year, as I took out boxes and looked for different items, instead of putting them back neatly in their assigned places, I set them in the middle of the room. One by one the boxes piled up. Now there's no path to walk, and I can't find anything.

Sometimes my life gets cluttered too. Just as I filled my attic during the course of the year, day by day I pack my schedule with plans. Most of them are worthwhile, but they may not necessarily be the plans God had in mind. I lose my sense of what's important. When I continue to pile one activity on another, I become so confused that I end up doing nothing. Only by taking time to pray and seek God's will can I maintain a clear view of what He wants me to do.

Prayer: Lord, help me to daily seek Your will for my life rather than allowing clutter to fill my mind. Amen.

Your View: Is your calendar overloaded with activities that keep you from focusing on God? What changes can you make so you can discern where He is leading you?

_____
_____
_____
_____
_____

CHAPTER 8

When Jesus Needs Us

First on My List

On top of my list
Of "things I must do"
Is spending an hour
Each day, God, with You.

My schedule is hectic
But I take time to pray,
For when I neglect You
My priorities stray.

It's hard to stay focused
Unless You're in control...
Too many distractions
To body and soul.

Help me to listen.
Help me be still.
My deepest desire...
To stay in Your will.

Watchful or Sleeping?

Read Matthew 26:36-45

"My soul is overwhelmed with sorrow to the point of death. Stay here and keep watch with me." Matthew 26:38

"What can I get you? How about tea and toast?" my husband asked.

Whenever I'm sick or experiencing a difficulty, I can always count on my husband, Jim, to comfort me. Just having him with me seems to alleviate my apprehension. People who live alone aren't that fortunate. When they're not well, they have no one to chat with or to get them whatever they need.

In Gethsemane, Jesus was overwhelmed with sorrow. He asked His disciples to stay near Him and keep an eye on what was happening. But when He needed them most, they closed their eyes and fell asleep—not once but three times. The ones Jesus counted on to keep watch disappointed Him.

I want to be available whenever Jesus needs me. My personal relationship with Him is the number one priority of my life. I want Him to know that He can always count on me.

Prayer: Lord, help me be attentive so I'll be wide awake when You need me. Amen.

Your View: How can you improve your relationship with Jesus so that you'll be awake when He needs you?

_____

_____

_____

_____

_____

CHAPTER 9
Following God's Directions

No Room for Satan

Does the devil stop at your house?
Well, he often stops at mine,
Especially when I'm happy
And things are going fine.

It makes him very angry
When he sees my faith is strong...
That I quickly turn to Jesus
When temptation comes along.

He tries to make me restless;
He tries to make me doubt.
He wants to fill my head with lies
And turn life inside out.

But God is always at my side;
He promised He would be.
I'm sheltered in His loving arms...
He's won the victory!

God's Directions Are Best

Read Psalm 119:33-40

Give me understanding, and I will keep your law and obey it with all my heart. Psalm 119:34

What should I do? I was accurately following the directions, but the map had not indicated a detour.

Although confused, I drove in what I thought was the right direction. Suddenly a highway sign caught my eye. I was going east instead of west. If I continued, I would go farther out of my way. So I turned around and stopped at a store to seek help. Equipped with the correct instructions, I finally reached my destination.

I have a map of plans for my life too. Each day I try to accomplish my goals, but when unexpected events change my plans, my perspective may become distorted. I wonder if these interruptions are divinely appointed detours from God or roadblocks set up by Satan to distract me?

When I'm unsure what to do, I stop and quietly look for direction from the Lord through prayer and Bible study. If I follow His instructions, I know I'll achieve my ultimate goal—living a life that pleases Him.

Prayer: Lord, help me to clearly see Your will for my life. Don't let me be misguided. Help me to discern whether the detours are from You or Satan. Amen.

Your View: How do you react when unexpected events change your plans? Do you jump to conclusions or do you look to God for direction?

_____
_____
_____
_____
_____

CHAPTER 10

Christ in Me

What Do People See, Lord?

Even if I face a crisis
Can my friends and family see
Your peace and joy and gentleness
Flowing out of me?

Do they notice that I trust in You
To guide and pull me through…
That no matter what is happening
I keep my eyes on You?

I hope my life will always be
A beacon of Your light,
So others, too, will trust in You
And walk by faith, not sight.

A Vessel for God's Use

Read Galatians 2:20-21

*Man looks at the outward appearance, but the Lord
looks at the heart.* 1 Samuel 16:7

While arranging a bouquet of rust-colored carnations in a crystal vase, I noticed that one of the stems was cracked and three tiny buds were clinging to the broken section. I was going to discard them, but instead I placed the buds in an empty plastic juice bottle I rescued from the recycling bin. The bottle wasn't very pretty, but once the flowers were in it, my eyes focused less on the container and more on the buds.

Looking at the makeshift vase on my counter the next day, I realized I had something in common with it. For many years, I was like that average-looking plastic bottle—empty and waiting to be filled. Then my son Brian told me about Jesus and His desire to have a personal relationship with me. When I asked Jesus into my life, I became a container for Him and felt blessed to be available for His use.

Just as my eyes were more attracted to the buds than to the plastic bottle, I pray that others will look beyond my outward appearance and be attracted to Christ living in me.

Prayer: Thank You, Lord, that what matters most to You is my heart. Amen.

Your View: Have you given your heart to the Lord? Are you experiencing His peace and joy?

_____
_____
_____
_____
_____

CHAPTER 11
Rekindling Our First Love

Do We Radiate God's Light to Others?

Do others see Christ living in us?
Do our lives point that He is the Way?
Do we radiate His love to others?
By the actions and words that we say?

Is His joy inscribed on our faces?
Do we share all the things that He's done?
Do we have a real hunger to witness
So that none will be lost—no not one?

Let's aim to draw others to Jesus
By the things that we do and we say.
Let's be a light in the darkness
To assure them that Christ is the Way.

Radiating God's Light

Read Psalm 51

Create in me a pure heart, O God, and renew a steadfast spirit within me. Psalm 51:10

I watched as my husband put crumpled newspaper under the logs in our wood stove. After he lit the paper, the flames wrapped themselves around the wood and danced brightly behind the glass doors, casting a soft glow on the walls. Heat quickly radiated throughout the room, and I soon fell asleep on the couch.

When I awoke, the flames were gone, but the logs were still glowing. I added another piece of wood, and in a short time, new flames brightened the room.

When I first met the Lord, I was on fire with my newfound love. My joyous heart danced, radiating God's light to others.

I still love the Lord, but from time to time I allow the fire of Christ's love to die out. But just as the fire in my wood stove is rekindled when logs are added, my spirit is revived when I fellowship with the Lord and spend time studying the Bible. He can restore the bright flames of His love that I experienced when I first invited Him into my heart.

Prayer: Lord, please continually rekindle my love for You and help me to radiate Your warmth and light to others. Amen.

Your View: How brightly are you radiating God's light? Devote ten minutes a day to reading God's Word and see what a brilliant difference it makes.

_____
_____
_____
_____
_____

CHAPTER 12
No Need to Fear

He Never Leaves Us

God promises not to leave us
Or withhold from us His care,
Yet at times it seems He's absent,
That He really is not there.

It looks like He is silent,
Hidden from our view,
Yet truly He is always there,
Helping to see us through.

Our Protector

Read Psalm 91:1-10

Those who trust in the Lord are like Mount Zion,
which cannot be shaken but endures forever. Psalm 125:1

On a hot humid morning, as I walked past a rippling stream, I spotted a mother duck and her ducklings waddling up the bank toward the wooden bridge. The mother duck moved slowly so her little ones could catch up to her. With head held high, she surveyed the area, looking cautiously from left to right to make sure the path was safe.

I stood only two feet from the ducks, yet they didn't scurry away. They continued their slow pace as if I weren't there. The babies evidently trusted that their mother had everything under control.

When I asked Jesus into my life, He took me under His wing. Through daily fellowship with Him and studying His Word, I have learned to trust Him with everything. Like the baby ducks, when unsettling circumstances invade my day, I'm not afraid, for Jesus, My Protector, promises never to leave nor forsake me.

What greater gift can I receive?

Prayer: Lord, how blessed we are that Your arms are always open to comfort and protect us. Help us to show that same love to others. Amen.

Your View: Are your eyes on Jesus or on unsettling circumstances today? What can you do to change your viewpoint?

_____
_____
_____
_____
_____

CHAPTER 13
Taking God Seriously

Help Me Be Still

Why must I always be busy?
Why can I never rest?
Why must I always be "doing"?
Whom do I need to impress?

I have a preconceived notion
That stillness is not a good sign;
If others see me just sitting,
Some fault in me they will find.

I seem to forget, dear Jesus,
That You always took time to be still,
That I must make time for silence,
If I'm ever to learn Your will.

Help me to change my old habits.
Teach me to slow down my pace.
Show me where I should be heading,
And fill me with Your loving grace.

Am I Paying Attention?

Read Deuteronomy 6:1-9

For the eyes of the Lord range throughout the earth to strengthen those whose hearts are fully committed to him. 2 Chronicles 16:9

As our car moved slowly up the hill, a flurry of movement caught my eye. It was a group of deer. Frightened by our headlights, they stood so still they looked like lawn ornaments. But as our car moved past them, the deer scurried away.

God's light often shines unexpectedly on us—sometimes through His Word, sometimes through events, and sometimes through other people. Often, He is trying to show us a better path. Other times He wants us to slow down so we have time to grow closer to Him.

How do we react when God reaches out to us? Do we take Christ's message to heart and act on it? Or do we pause for just a minute, as the deer did, and then hurry back to what we were doing?

Prayer: Lord, don't allow me to get so busy that I have no time for You. Instead, prompt me stop what I'm doing, focus on You, and listen to what You say. Amen.

Your View: Have the headlights of God's truth stopped you lately? What do you think He is saying to you?

_____

_____

_____

_____

_____

CHAPTER 14
Our Own Flaws First

Why, God?

Why do I think that if others would change
Life would be happier for me?
Why do I always judge their faults,
But my own I somehow don't see?

Why don't I ever stop to think
That if I'd change, perhaps they might too?
Why don't I first take a look at myself,
And leave changing them up to You!

More Like Christ

Read Matthew 7:1-5

Why do you look at the speck of sawdust in your brother's eye and pay no attention to the plank in your own eye? Matthew 7:3

"You missed a spot," I informed the painter, as I watched him paint my living room. He quickly touched it up, but I'm sure he didn't appreciate my eyeing his every move. I have a habit of checking on other workers that I hire, and I supervise my husband too. Yet, I don't like anyone doing that to me.

How blessed I am that God doesn't point His finger at me every time I slip up. If God judged what I do as I often judge what others do, I would be in serious trouble.

Why do we see the imperfections and failures of others more than our own? Wouldn't it be better to work on changing ourselves, and let God take care of other people?

Let's be more like Christ and extend to others the grace that He extends to us.

Prayer: Lord, help me see people with compassionate eyes rather than critical ones. Help me to diligently work on correcting my faults and bad habits and allow You to change other people. Amen.

Your View: Who do you judge most critically? How can you extend grace to that person?

_____
_____
_____
_____
_____

CHAPTER 15
A Spiritual Flashlight

In the Light

Many years I walked in darkness;
Now I'm walking in the light.
Pain and struggle were required
So I might gain God's insight.

Though, at times, I could have yielded
To the devil and his plan,
I am grateful for the wisdom
I gleaned from the great I AM.

Perpetual Light

Read Psalm 119:97-105

You are my lamp, Oh Lord; the Lord turns my darkness into light. 2 Samuel 22:29

My husband always keeps a flashlight nearby. He keeps one in his car, one by the bed, two by his recliner, and several in the cellar. He even has a small one on his key chain.

I used to tease him about having so many. *Who needs them,* I thought. Yet when there is a power failure or when he needs to look for something in a dimly lit or obscure place, he is always prepared.

God provides a spiritual flashlight for all of us—the Bible. Psalm 119:105 assures us that God's Word is a lamp to our feet and a light for our path.

For most of my life, I didn't know about God's light. When I discovered the Bible, it changed my life dramatically. Its words enlightened me, and I gleaned knowledge of God beyond my wildest expectations.

Studying Scripture and memorizing God's promises are priorities in my life. I treasure my Bible as my daily flashlight. With God's Word in my heart and on my tongue, I too am prepared for any situation.

Prayer: Lord, fill me to overflowing with Your Holy Spirit so others will see You in me. Use me to shed Your light wherever I go. Amen.

Your View: How has God's Word provided light for you? With whom can you share that light?

_____

_____

_____

_____

_____

CHAPTER 16
Is My Name There?

Our Decision

Through trials and heartaches,
Sickness and pain,
There's One who upholds us
With His precious name.
Jesus!
He lifts all our burdens,
Lightens each care;
When we call out His name,
He always is there.
Jesus!
He never forsakes us,
He stays at our side.
Though at times He seems silent,
His arms open wide.
Jesus!
He continues to love us
In spite of our sin,
But it's we who decide
If we'll welcome Him in.

A Permanent Record

Read Revelation 3:1-6

I will never blot out his name from the book of life.
Revelation 3:5

Have you ever seen an autograph book? They were popular in the 1940s when I was in grammar school.

At the end of each school year, I bought a new book. My friends signed their names and wrote about events and fun times we had experienced together. Some classmates composed poems and others included jokes. At that time, I cherished those books and looked at them often during my summer vacations. But when I entered high school, I discarded them. I wish I had kept some of them. Now all of those memories are gone.

Jesus has a unique kind of autograph book—the Lamb's Book of Life. No one has seen it, and only He can write in it. Best of all, He promises never to throw it away.

When we accept Jesus as Lord and Savior, He excitedly engraves our names in His everlasting Book of Life and assures us that our names will be visible to Him forever.

Prayer: Father, I pray that all those who hear of Jesus will accept Him as Lord and Savior so their names will be permanently engraved in the Lamb's Book of Life. Amen.

Your View: Have you accepted Jesus as your Lord and Savior? Does He see your name in The Lamb's Book of Life when He reads it? How does that make you feel?

_____

_____

_____

_____

_____

CHAPTER 17
The Holy Spirit – Our Helper

More Like You

Today, Lord, I feel like violin strings
Being tuned.
With each twist of Your fingers,
You adjust the tension
As You stretch me
To be more in harmony with Your will.
I want to say, "Stop!"
But Your Word says
You refine those You love.
How blessed I am
That You care enough
To fine-tune me
To sound more like You.

Layer by Layer

Read Hebrews 12:4-11

Because the Lord disciplines those he loves, as a father the son he delights in. Proverbs 3:12

What a painstaking job! I was struggling to strip paint off my old-fashioned, freestanding bathroom radiator. I could see from the chips and layers of paint that it had been painted many times.

I should have chosen a stronger chemical with toxic fumes, but instead I had selected a gentle one that wouldn't endanger my health. This made the process more tedious, yet after days of scraping I could see the progress I was making.

Though God forgives us our sins when we repent, we still have an accumulation of bad habits that need to be removed. God could use strong methods of chastising us. Instead, He uses the gentle nudging of His Holy Spirit to convict us. He points out our faults through Scripture, through written material, and through people. He then gives us His strength to overcome our weaknesses.

Stripping us of our bad habits is a tedious job, too, but after God patiently works with us and changes us, others will see the progress He has made.

Prayer: Lord, thank You for caring enough to convict us and to help us overcome our sins. How fortunate we are to have a God who sees what is best for us. Amen.

Your View: How do you react when the Holy Spirit convicts you of a bad habit? How does God want you to respond?

_____

_____

_____

_____

_____

CHAPTER 18
Are We Tuned In?

My Sovereign Guide

I am refreshed, dear Jesus,
By the little things You do.
You speak to me in different ways
But I always know it's You.

Today I heard a serenade
When I awoke at dawn,
And I still felt Your presence
After the songbirds had gone.

You often send me rainbows
When sun reflects on glass.
In troubling times, they speak to me,
"This too, my child, shall pass."

Sometimes a word pops off the page
While I'm spending time with You.
Your Word shines light upon my path,
Confirms what I'm to do.

You always know what's best for me;
I trust Your perfect plan.
I'm blessed that You're my Sovereign Guide,
The Awesome, Great I AM.

Touched by the Spirit

Read Romans 5:6-11

While we were still sinners, Christ died for us.
Romans 5:8

While drying my hands in our church restroom, I spotted a large wad of dirty, crumpled paper towels on the floor. I considered picking it up, but after taking a second look, I thought, *Why should I touch that?*

I walked out, leaving the towels where they were. But as the door closed behind me, the Holy Spirit's words prompted me to return: *Jesus picked you up when you were dirty from your sins. He didn't leave you where you were. He took your sins and those of the world upon Himself and nailed them to the cross so that you would have eternal life.*

With my head shamefully bowed, I humbly turned around and opened the bathroom door. With a renewed frame of mind, I willingly picked up the dirty towels and gratefully thanked the Lord for not turning His back on me.

It always amazes me how God turns a simple everyday experience into a learning lesson. My part is to keep my eyes and ears open so I won't miss His teaching or His blessings.

Prayer: Jesus, thank You for sending Your Holy Spirit to teach us to look at things from Your perspective. Amen.

Your View: Are you tuned in to the Holy Spirit's guidance? What spiritual analogy could you draw from a recent experience?

_____

_____

_____

_____

_____

CHAPTER 19
Do My Actions Point to Jesus?

God's Perfect Peace

On days when I feel shackled
Let me not forget I'm free...
That You took my sins and nailed them
To the cross at Calvary.

My old ways and bad habits
Were washed clean the day You died.
Forgive me when I cling to them
For that's the sin of pride.

And when I try to run my life
Instead of trusting You,
Again forgive me, Jesus,
For that's not the thing to do.

You said Your yoke is easy
And that Your burden's light,
So there's no valid reason
Why I should get uptight.

So help me, Lord, to rest in You,
May others always see
Your abiding perfect peace
Pouring out of me.

What Signals Am I Giving?

Read Galatians 5:16-26

But the fruit of the spirit is love, joy, peace, patience, kindness, goodness, faithfulness, gentleness and self-control. Galatians 5:22-23

Directional signals on a car can be confusing! Sometimes a driver puts on his right signal but turns left. Other times a driver puts on the directional signal but never turns at all. It's difficult to know how to react when what you see in front of you may not be accurate. Many accidents occur because of improper signals.

When we profess to be Christians, people observe the signals we give. They watch to see if our actions measure up to our words. Are we exemplifying the fruit of the Spirit listed in Galatians 5:22-23? If we tell others that they should obey God but don't live that way ourselves, we send out mixed messages.

Paying attention to the signals that we're giving to others ensures that we don't cause spiritual accidents.

Prayer: Lord, help me to stay in Your Word and obey Your commandments so others will see You in me. Amen.

Your View: What kind of signals do you give to those around you? Can they count on you to point them toward Jesus?

_____
_____
_____
_____
_____

CHAPTER 20
Deny You? Never!

Despite the Cost

The hour is late!
The time draws near!
Before Christ comes,
The world must hear
That He's the Way,
The Truth, the Life...
That He alone,
Brings peace, not strife.

So I must write
Despite the cost...
To spread God's Word,
To reach the lost.
I must not faint
When some say "no,"
I must keep on...
God's Word, I'll sow.

And when I meet
Christ face to face,
I pray He'll say,
"Well done! Good race!"

Not Me!

Read Matthew 26:69-75

But Peter declared, "Even if I have to die with you, I will never disown you." Matthew 26:35

A paper airplane whizzed through the classroom and hit the corner of Mrs. Smith's eye before landing on her desk. Shocked by the sudden arrival of the plane, she jumped to her feet.

"Who did that?" she demanded. No one answered.

The pupils in the front had no idea who was responsible, but the students in the back row had seen Jeremy throw it. When Mrs. Smith asked the question again, Jeremy still didn't admit that he was the one who had hurled the airplane toward the front of the classroom. Denial came easily. He didn't want to get in trouble.

When Jesus told Peter that before the cock crowed he would deny Jesus three times, Peter was quick to say, "Not me!" But later, when Peter was questioned about his association with Jesus, three times he denied that he had been with Him. Maybe he feared that he too would be arrested and put on trial.

Lying is a sin. Let's not allow it into our lives.

Prayer: Jesus, help me never to be afraid to tell others how much I love You. In Your precious name, amen.

Your View: How do you react when questioned about your relationship with Jesus? Are you proud of your association with Him, or do you hesitate to admit that you are His disciple?

_____

_____

_____

_____

_____

CHAPTER 21
Our First Priority

Help Me to Prioritize

There are so many distractions, Lord,
That keep me from hearing You.
E-mail, Facebook, phone calls, housework...
Just to name a few.
All very time consuming.
Help me to prioritize and sit quietly
At Your feet with no distractions.
Then I will clearly hear Your still, small voice.

Setting Priorities

Read Exodus 18

"What you are doing is not good...the work is too heavy for you: you cannot handle it alone." Exodus 18:17-18

I plugged in my coffee pot, put bread in the toaster, and started to open a can of fruit with my electric can opener. Suddenly the power went off. Fortunately, I saw the problem—too many appliances on one circuit.

I reset the circuit breaker and moved my toaster to another socket on the other side of the room. When the load was divided among several sockets, all of the appliances functioned as they were designed to, and I had a peaceful breakfast.

Like my electrical system, at times I also burn out. When I look at my schedule and see that it is overloaded with too many activities, I become physically and mentally exhausted before I even begin. When I try to do three things at once, Jesus reminds me that only one thing is really needed—time for Him.

Now when I feel overburdened, I reset my priorities. I seek the Lord in prayer and rearrange my schedule to make sure that I have included time for Him. When I do, I'm able to function as God designed me to. Then and only then do I truly experience His peace that passes all understanding.

Prayer: Lord, keep reminding me that You want to be my number one priority. Amen.

Your View: What does your calendar look like? What changes do you need to make in order to experience God's peace?

_____

_____

_____

_____

_____

CHAPTER 22
Faith, Not Works

Eternal Assurance

The cross lay bare and bloodstained...
The nails ripped from Christ's hands.
They came and took His body.
Most did not understand.

The crowd wept tears of sorrow
For they did not realize
His mission was accomplished...
In three days He would arise.

What seemed like such a tragedy
Was all part of God's plan.
When Jesus died, He paid the price...
Our sacrificial lamb.

He conquered death by rising
And opened heaven's door.
If we will just believe in Him,
Our destiny's secure.

Assurance

Read Ephesians 2:1-9

For it is by grace you have been saved, through faith—
not by works, so that no one can boast. Ephesians 2:8-9

I turned my new oven dials to the clean cycle and set the clock for three hours. So simple compared to my old stove. I used to spray the interior with chemicals, leave them on several hours, then put on rubber gloves and scrub vigorously until my oven looked new. The fumes were harsh on my eyes and nose, and my back ached from kneeling on the floor, but the result was worth it.

Now, in three hours, I open the door of my self-cleaning oven and see a spotless interior. No effort on my part required.

Years ago, I struggled with guilt and condemnation. Would I ever envision my life clean enough to be worthy of salvation? I had been taught that I had to work to obtain God's forgiveness of my sins.

Now I know the truth. In three hours on the cross, the same time it takes to produce a spotless oven, Jesus permanently cleansed my sins. If I accept His gift of salvation, I am assured of eternal life.

Prayer: Thank You, Lord, for opening my eyes to Your free gift of salvation. Amen.

Your View: Do you still struggle with trying to earn your salvation? Ephesians 2:8-9 assures us that we are saved by faith.

_____

_____

_____

_____

_____

CHAPTER 23
Walking in Unison

Nurture Me, Lord

*Fill me
With the rich soil
Of Your Word.
Plant in me
Seeds of kindness,
Goodness and love.
Drench me
With Your living water
That I may grow
In Your image
And bloom
Forever
In Your heavenly garden.*

No Greater Reward

Read John 17:20-23

For in him we live and move and have our being.
Acts 17:28

I love to watch couples ice skate in competitions. The best pairs skate in unison, as if they were one. They anticipate each other's moves and rarely make a mistake. To reach this stage of excellence, they spend countless hours practicing. They also accept continual criticism and correction from their coaches. But their hard work pays off when they receive recognition from the judges and the crowd.

God wants us to walk in unison with Him. Just as He and the Father are one, He wants us to be one with Him. To become like Him also takes practice. Just as the skaters study each other's moves, we must study God's Word to learn how He moves and acts so we can become like Him. We must also be willing to accept criticism and correction from the Lord. But our reward for being one with Him is far greater than a skater's medal or trophy—we will spend eternity with Him in heaven.

Prayer: Thank You, Lord, for patiently teaching me how to be like You. Help me to be a willing student. Amen.

Your View: Are you moving in unison with God? Describe your relationship with Him.

_____

_____

_____

_____

_____

CHAPTER 24
The Most Important Meal

A Different Kind of Diet

I recently discovered
A different kind of diet.
I hope that when you read about it
You will want to try it.

It nourishes your spirit,
Gives your face a special glow;
It reaches deep into your soul
So peace and joy will grow.

Just set aside ten minutes
On your calendar each day,
For time alone with Jesus
To worship Him and pray.

Cast all your cares upon Him;
He'll lighten up your load.
With Him in charge of all you do
You'll walk a smoother road.

Soon you'll find you crave more time
Instead of wanting less.
A daily diet of God's Word
Is guaranteed to bless.

God's Table

Read Proverbs 3:1-8

Do not be wise in your own eyes; fear the Lord and shun evil. This will bring health to your body and nourishment to your bones. Proverbs 3:7-8

My husband, Jim, sets a beautiful table on our back deck. It isn't the usual table meant for dishes and silverware; this one displays a variety of unusually shaped bird feeders, each filled with a different kind of seed.

New Jersey's state bird, the goldfinch, frequently visits us for a snack. Red-winged blackbirds, red poles, sparrows, and cardinals occasionally stop for a meal.

It's fun to watch their tactics. The small birds peck a little at a time; they're in no hurry. The larger birds swoop in, gobble up the seeds, and quickly fly away.

God sets an even more beautiful table. Throughout the Bible, He offers a splendid variety of spiritual food for our souls—simple truths for beginners who need easily digestible meals and deeper, meatier selections for more seasoned Christians to savor.

Why do we often neglect God's offer of spiritual nourishment?

Jim and I get excited when birds visit our feeders. Imagine how much more delighted God is when we come to His table.

Prayer: Father, may we always take time to eat with You. Your food is the only kind that offers lasting nourishment. Amen.

Your View: How often do you take advantage of God's nourishment? Is your Bible getting dusty?

_____

_____

_____

_____

_____

CHAPTER 25

A Better Agenda

A Perfect Picture

Life is like a puzzle
We can't understand;
The pieces don't fit
When they're placed by our hand.

But when God takes the pieces
And puts them in place,
They fit smoothly together
Because of His grace.

For He knows how He made us
And what we're to do,
Plus the timing is perfect
From His point of view.

The Master Planner

Read Isaiah 55:6-11

For my thoughts are not your thoughts, neither are
your ways my ways, declares the Lord. Isaiah 55:8

"Keep 9:30 tomorrow morning free," Jim informed me. "We have an appointment with the accountant."

Not again! Three meetings in one week. First the lawyer, then the financial advisor, and now this. My husband's plans disrupted my schedule.

"I have things I'd rather do," I mumbled, yet I knew that getting Jim's retirement papers in order was important.

Often God's plans for me seem inconvenient too. Even though I have released my life to the Lord, my human nature still wants its own way.

God's interruptions sometimes come in the form of a sudden illness, unexpected company, a separation, or just a simple turn of events. When these things occur, I can be annoyed, or I can accept them. When I react without praying, I usually regret my decision. When I accept God's agenda, I discover His plans are always better than mine. He is looking out for my best interests. I only see bits and pieces of the future. God sees the whole picture.

Prayer: Lord, help me to look at every situation through Your eyes and rest in You. Remind me that Your ways are better than mine. Amen.

Your View: Think of a time when you were inconvenienced. How could you have handled the situation better?

_____
_____
_____
_____
_____

CHAPTER 26
Don't Give Up!

Because He Lives

O, dear heavenly Father,
We come boldly to Your throne,
Through the blood of Jesus
By nothing of our own.

For Jesus opened heaven's door
When He died on the cross,
And three days later rose again
So none need to be lost.

How blessed we are...He bridged the gap
Left open by man's sin.
How blessed we are...because of Him
That we can enter in.

Despite the Circumstances

Read Psalm 23

We live by faith, not by sight. 2 Corinthians 5:7

It's easy to believe in God when life is going well, but when we are confronted with challenging circumstances, the sincerity of our faith is tested.

Raising five boys, all born within six years, was an eye-opening challenge for me, to say the least! The teenage years especially were a blur of activity—many good times, but many difficult times as well.

I often felt overwhelmed and wondered, *How will I be able to handle my God-given responsibilities without caving in?* But I never gave up. Despite those trying years, with the Lord's help, I survived and so did my boys.

My hard times were nothing compared to the trials Jesus faced when He headed to the cross. Despite His anguish, He never took His eyes off the reason He came. Instead He prayed, "My Father, if it is not possible for this cup to be taken away unless I drink it, may your will be done" (Matthew 26:42).

Because Jesus endured death on the cross and rose again, we can live forever too. Believing that His sacrifice cleanses our sins and restores our relationship with the Father is our guarantee. That confidence can keep our faith strong in all circumstances.

Prayer: Jesus, knowing that I will see You face to face is what keeps me going. I pray that You will continue to be glorified in my circumstances. Amen.

Your View: When your faith is tested, how do you react?

_____
_____
_____
_____
_____

CHAPTER 27
A Joyous Focus

Distractions

D *ifficulty concentrating*
I *mmobilizing my mind*
S *anity disrupted*
T *hinking distorted*
R *unning in circles*
A *nxiety setting in*
C *onfusion increasing*
T *ension mounting*
I *nvading my schedule*
O *ut of control*
N *ot the way to live*
S *top it!*

What Grabs Your Attention?

Read Hebrews 12: 1-3

Let us fix our eyes on Jesus, the author and perfecter of our faith, who for the joy set before him endured the cross, scorning its shame, and sat down at the right hand of the throne of God. Hebrews 12:2

While watching TV one day, I was distracted by a black spot moving up and down on the screen. Though I tried to stay focused on my program, my eyes were continually drawn to the movement.

Suddenly, I realized that a tiny spider was climbing up and down a web that was invisible from where I sat. Because I let that industrious insect capture my attention, I missed most of my program.

Too often, I let the distractions of everyday activities take my focus off of Jesus. When that happens, I get sidetracked and make plans without first consulting Him. I end up missing many of the blessings God wants to give me.

In Matthew 6:33, Jesus said, "But seek first his kingdom and his righteousness, and all these things will be given to you as well." If I put Christ first, He promises to supply all my needs. Shouldn't that motivate me to keep my eyes firmly focused on Him?

Prayer: Jesus, You are the way, the truth and the life. Capture my attention so that my eyes will be drawn to You. Amen.

Your View: What diverts your attention from God? How can you eliminate those distractions?

_____
_____
_____
_____
_____

CHAPTER 28
A Compelling Light

Only Jesus

Who knows each moment how you feel?
Whose love for you is always real?
Who cares for you and guides your way?
Who holds your hand so you won't stray?

Jesus!

Who's there when others turn their backs?
Who helps you get your life on track?
Who always wants to be your friend?
On whom alone can you depend?

Jesus!

Who's there for you both day and night?
Who soothes your pain and makes things right?
Who walked the road to Calvary
And gave His life, so you'd be free?

Jesus!

Who is Our Savior and Our King,
Our Counselor—Our Everything?

Only Jesus!

Let Your Light Shine

Read Matthew 22:37-38

Therefore encourage one another and build each other up. 1 Thessalonians 5:11

Recently, we had a power failure. The lights suddenly went out. Usually power is restored within a half hour, but that night it didn't come on for five hours. During the dark hours, I read for a while by candlelight and also spent time talking with my husband, Jim. It was actually quite enjoyable with no phone and TV interruptions.

We take so many things for granted. We presume that the electricity, water, and other necessities will always be available. We forget that glitches can happen, often at the most inconvenient times. But there is Someone that we can always count on. He's available twenty-four hours a day. Are we available for Him?

Today, many people have taken God out of their lives altogether. They no longer consider consulting Him for any of their decisions. Let's be among those who give Him first place in our lives, as He does with us. May others observe how we live and be drawn closer to Christ.

Prayer: Lord, help me to stay focused on You so that I won't take Your blessings for granted. Amen.

Your View: What can you do to make yourself more available to God? How can you draw others to Him?

_____
_____
_____
_____
_____

CHAPTER 29
Always Amazing

My Faithful Lord

You promised to love me,
You promised to care.
Though at times You seem absent,
I know You are there.

You've given me love,
You've given me hope,
You hold my hand often,
You've helped me to cope.

I must not forget You,
I must remain true,
For there's no one who loves me
As much as You do.

An Unexpected View

Read Proverbs 3:13-18

The eye is the lamp of the body. If your eyes are good,
your whole body will be full of light. Matthew 6:22

I was tempted to cancel my scheduled cataract surgery. The thought of having my eye cut and the doctor implanting a new lens in my right eye made me squeamish. But the cataract was clouding my vision, and my doctor said the operation was necessary.

After awaking from surgery, I had to wear a patch on my eye overnight, so I couldn't check the results.

The following morning when the doctor removed the patch, I noticed a dramatic change. When I read the chart, she was exceptionally pleased. The vision in my right eye was 20/20.

I still needed a slight adjustment for my left eye and reading lenses, but I would have to wait a few weeks before wearing my new prescription. In the meantime, I was enjoying a new perspective of the world without glasses.

That experience reminded me of my walk with God. I always loved Him, but when I got to know Him personally, my life changed dramatically. Once I invited Jesus to be my personal Savior and Lord, I started to see everything differently.

Just as my physical eyesight improved after my surgery, passages in the Bible that I didn't understand became clearer after my spiritual eyesight was corrected. Now I have 20/20 eyesight and 20/20 spiritual vision.

Prayer: Lord, thank You for Your surprise blessings and Your continual faithfulness. Amen.

Your View: Do you read the Bible regularly? Are its messages clear to you?

_____

_____

_____

_____

_____

CHAPTER 30
An Eternal Guarantee

There Still Is Time

Jesus could have died alone,
But on the hill hung three.
Perhaps it was God's message
For all of us to see...

There still is time, while we're alive
To acknowledge all our sin.
If we'll repent, He will forgive
And come to live within.

Yet only one man at His side
Admitted he should die.
The other chose to jeer and mock...
His guilt, he did deny.

So Jesus showed His mercy
To the sinner who was wise,
And spoke the words, "You'll be with me
Today in paradise."

God wants us all to join Him too
But He won't raise His voice
Or pressure us to take that step...
Salvation is our choice.

Don't Wait!

Read Mark 13:24-37

No one knows about that day or hour, not even the angels in heaven, nor the Son, but only the Father. Mark 13:32

"The oatmeal I bought yesterday is half price today," my husband said as he showed me the weekly circular.

"We should've waited," I chimed in. "I see that the cold cereal you purchased is also half price."

At first, I was disappointed, but then I realized that we can't be sure when something will go on sale. Besides, we were out of cereal, and we didn't want to wait.

Waiting often brings rewards, and doing research before purchasing saves money, but there is one decision we should never put off—accepting Jesus as our personal Savior.

We don't need to wait for salvation to go on sale. Jesus already paid the price. It is ours for the asking. "If you confess with your mouth 'Jesus is Lord' and believe in your heart that God raised him from the dead, you will be saved" (Romans 10:9).

When we miss a sale, we may lose a few dollars, but we can always purchase the items another day. If we put off inviting Christ into our life, like the unrepentant thief on the cross, our loss would be much greater. We'd miss the opportunity to spend eternity with Him.

Prayer: Thank You, Lord, for offering us the security of knowing that we can spend eternity with You if we will accept You as Lord and Savior. Amen.

Your View: Have you been waiting to make a decision about your relationship with Jesus Christ? Is He both your Savior and Lord?

_____

_____

_____

_____

_____

DOUBLE VISION – EYE FACTS

- Your eyes are composed of more than two million working parts. They are the most complex organs except for the brain.

- The average person blinks twelve times per minute—about ten thousand blinks in an average day. Blinking helps to wash tears over our eyeballs.

- Only one-sixth of our eyeball is visible in the outside world.

- Less than 1 percent of the population is born with two different color eyes. This is called heterochromia.

- It is impossible to sneeze with your eyes open.

- The clear cornea at the front of the eye is the only living tissue in the human body that doesn't contain any blood vessels.

- Under the right conditions the eye can see the light of a candle at a distance of fourteen miles.

- Color blindness is ten times more common in males than females. Red and green are the most commonly confused colors among color-blind people. All babies are born color-blind.

- The eye is the only part of the human body that can function at 100 percent ability at any moment, day or night, without rest.

- The eyeball of a human weighs approximately twenty-eight grams.

- People generally read 25 percent slower from a computer screen than from paper.

- The human eye can distinguish between five hundred shades of grey and can detect over ten million colors.

- The lens of the eye allows us to focus on different things. It changes shape so we can focus on objects of various sizes.

- The pupil is the central opening of your eye. It changes size depending on the amount of light.

- The iris is the colored area around the pupil. It controls the size of the pupil and it can be various shades of brown, blue, or green.

- Eyes do not wear out. You can use them as much as you want.

- The number one cause of blindness in adults in the United States is diabetes.

- 80 percent of vision problems worldwide are avoidable or even curable.

- Each of your eyes has a small blind spot in the back of the retina where the optic nerve attaches. You don't notice the hole in your vision because your eyes work together to fill in each other's blind spot.

- Sailors once thought that wearing a gold earring would improve their eyesight.

- The older we get the fewer tears we produce.

- The shark cornea has been used in eye surgery since it is similar to a human cornea.

- Eyebrows are meant to keep sweat from running into our eyes. Eyelashes help to keep dirt out of our eyes. Eyelashes have an average life span of five months.

- Men are able to read fine print better than women can.

- The eye can process 36,000 bits of information every hour.

- The most active muscles in your whole body are your eye muscles.

- Babies' eyes do not produce tears when they cry until the baby is approximately one to three months old.

- The human eye will focus on about fifty things per second.

- A newborn baby sees the world upside down because it takes some time for the baby's brain to learn to turn the picture right side up.

- Human eyes contribute toward 85 percent of your total knowledge.

Made in the USA
Lexington, KY
20 December 2013